SOR

SELECTED WORKS for GUITAR

EDITED AND FINGERED BY MARC TEICHOLZ

AN ALFRED CLASSICAL GUITAR MASTERWORKS EDITION

Cover art: a detail of
A View of Paris with the Île de la Cité
by Nicolas Jean Baptiste Raguenet (1715–1793)
Oil on canvas, 1763
The J. Paul Getty Museum, Los Angeles

Back cover photo of Marc Teicholz
by Oksana Teicholz

Alfred Music
P.O. Box 10003
Van Nuys, CA 91410-0003
alfred.com

ISBN-10: 1-4706-1777-3
ISBN-13: 978-1-4706-1777-6

FERNANDO SOR

Contents

Selected Works

Edited by Marc Teicholz

Fernando Sor

Fernando Sor (translations of his name include Josep Ferran Sorts i Muntades, Joseph Fernando Macari Sors, Ferran Sor, Ferdinand Sor, and Ferdinando Sor.) was born in Barcelona on February 14, 1778 and educated at the monastery of Montserrat near Barcelona. Due to his political affiliations, he was forced to leave Spain. He first lived in Paris, then London, later Russia (he followed a French ballerina there), and, finally back again, in Paris. It was here, during his retirement, that he composed the majority of his guitar works. Although many of these works are rich and varied, he often complained that the demands of the public frustrated his compositional ambitions and forced him to produce simple, nice-sounding pieces that didn't require any special technical ability. His bitterness towards his career during his final decade is palpable. For example, Op, 43 is entitled Mes Ennuis ("My Annoyances"), and six of his ballets are dedicated to "whoever wants them." The foreword to Op.45 morbidly says, "Let's see if that's that. Composed and dedicated to the person with the least patience, by Fernando Sor. Opus 45." His last work was a mass in honor of his daughter, Caroline, who died in 1837. Her death sent the already sickly Sor into serious depression, and he died of tongue and throat cancer on July 10, 1839.

His compositions for guitar include sonatas, studies, sets of variations, divertissements, easy pieces for beginners, and duets. He also composed extensively for opera, orchestra, string quartet, piano, voice (he was himself a very fine singer), and ballet (his ballet score Cendrillon (Cinderella) was extraordinarily popular.) He was generally regarded to be one of the greatest guitarists of his age. His guitar music is considered today to be a canonical part of our repertory.

I recommend that for those of you who want to learn more about this intrepid and important composer to read Brian Jeffery's book: *Fernando Sor: Composer and Guitarist*, second edition, Tecla Editions, 1994.

I particulary like Julian Bream's sensitive comment regarding Sor's charming musical style:

"I think Fernando Sor does have to be played with respect but for a certain type of innocence in his music. I think to over apply romanticism to the music is a great mistake. There is a classicism for example not unlike Mozart in his style which to my mind is a style of beautiful understatement. But if you give understatement space and time, it has a positive element that transcends the simplicity or the innocence of the material. Sor needs immense care and affection, and if one invests his music with that, I can't see how anybody can object to it."

Andante Largo from Six Petite Pieces, Op. 5

Although Sor's Andante Largo is from his Op. 5 "Six very easy little pieces," the piece is fairly challenging nonetheless. Here Sor offers two exceptionally beautiful contrasting themes. It is easy to imagine a group of woodwinds playing the innocent major theme followed by the strings for the dark, pulsating minor theme of the B section.

Largo from Fantasy No. 2 in C Minor, Op. 7

This is probably one of the most serious pieces of Sor's output for the guitar. It originally served as the extended introduction of a long and relatively conventional set of theme and variations but its musical power has allowed it to stand on its own. Strangely, it was originally written in a grand staff (perhaps indicating Sor's commitment to meticulous voice leading) and, probably for this reason, was rarely performed.

Introduction & Variations on a Theme by Mozart, Op. 9

This most deservedly famous of Sor's variations was first published in London in 1821 with the generous title: "The Favorite Air "Oh Cara armonia" from Mozart's Opera Il Flauto Magico, arranged with an Introduction and Variations for the Guitar, as performed by the Author at the Nobilities Concerts, dedicated to his brother (Carlos) by F. Sor." The theme of the work is in itself a slight variation of an aria at the end of Act I of Mozart's "The Magic Flute" entitled "Das klinget so herrlich." Sor may have used the Italian translation of the aria for his florid title but, interestingly, it was the English setting of the Aria (which when translated to "Away with Melancholy" was forced to change the melody's rhythm to accommodate the new lyrics) that Sor copied verbatim.

This piece may have suffered a bit over the years from overexposure but it is worth reminding ourselves of the work's enormously playful charm as well as its fresh, unhakneyed approach to the variation form. Each variation appears as a complete surprise from the last.

A few details need to be mentioned:

1. In the theme, I offered an alternate set of fingerings for the repeats (I did the same for the 1st half

of Variation 2). These are entirely optional (as are all my fingerings). There are, in fact, many more possibilites. For example, in bar 5 of the Theme, some guitarists use pulloffs on the 1st string (from "B" to "E") to good comic effect.

2. In bar 1 of Variation 1, I replace the first "F♯" with a "F𝄪." I could be wrong about this but many guitarists do the same and I prefer it.

3. In bar 14 of the coda, I recommend that you play the "D" with a harmonic on the 12th fret of the 4th string. Again, it doesn't say to do this in the original score but I find it irresistible. It is up to you!

Sonata "Grand Solo" in D Major, Op. 14

This is Sor at his most flamboyant and virtuosic. After a brooding melodramatic introduction, the piece explodes with energy and excitement requiring a player's utmost pizzazz. This would also be a good time to confess that this edition is not a scholarly one. The Grand Solo, for example, survives in a handful of different editions (Meissonnier, Castro, Aguado, for example) and rather than try to discover the most "authoritative" version, I simply cherry-picked the bits that I liked the best. In fact, although I do include the flashy passage in this edition, I actually prefer Julian Bream's fabulous recorded version which cuts out bars 187 to 211.

Theme & Variations on the Folias and Minuet

Patriotism may have inspired Sor to use the theme from his native country but the music appears to have originated in Portugal (it is characterized by the chord progression i-V7-i-VII-III-VII-i-V7-i) and was very much in vogue. Over 150 composers have used it in their works: from Lully to Vivaldi and Handel to Beethoven and, later Lizst, Rachmaninov, and even Llobet and Ponce. This turbulent set of Variations concludes peacefully with a seraphic minuet.

Sonata in C Major, Op. 15b

This energetic piece bustles along with the humor and optimism of a Haydn String quartet. It was published by Castro in 1810 or shortly before and therefore dates from Sor's Spanish period. Castro gave it no opus number, and called it "Sonata Seconda," having called the Grand Solo, Op. 14, "Sonata Prima." It was also later published by Meissonnier circa 1817–22 with the opus number 15. This piece could be programmed very effectively as a companion piece to the Largo, Op. 7 (which would otherwise leave the listener hanging in suspense over an unresolved dominant chord.)

Introduction & Variations on "Marlborough s'en va-t-en-guerre," Op. 28

"Marlbrough s'en va-t-en guerre" ("Marlborough Has Left for the War") was one of the most popular french folk songs. This sad tune was based on a false report of the death of John Churchill, 1st Duke of Marlborough (1650–1722) during the Battle of Malplaquet (one of the bloodiest battles in the 18th century) on September 11th in 1709. It tells how Marlborough's wife, awaiting his return from battle, is given the news of her husband's death.

The hearty melody is also used for "For he's a jolly good fellow" and "The bear went over the mountain" and probably predated the song's lyrics. The song was all the rage throughout Europe (and even Russia) and its name could be found all through daily life including written on soups, fans, porcelains, and toys.

The first verse, written below, translates roughly to "Marlborough has gone to war, rat-a-tat, rat-a-tat, rat-a-tat, doesn't know when he will come back."

Marlbrough s'en va-t-en guerre,
mironton, mironton, mirontaine,
Marlbrough s'en va-t-en guerre,
Ne sait quand reviendra.

Fantasy & Variations on the Scottish Air "Ye Banks and Braes," Op. 40

Fantasy & Variations on the Scottish Air "Ye Banks and Braes o' Bonnie Doune" Op. 40 (c1829–30) was based on a popular traditional Scottish tune "The Caledonian Hunt's delight." Scottish culture was something of a romantic fascination at the time (famous examples include Sir Walter Scott's wildly popular novels, Mendlessohn's *Scottish Symphony* and Donizetti's *Lucia di Lammermoor*) so it is possible that Sor was reacting to a fashionable trend. The words (printed below) to the tune were written by Robert Burns and its subject suggests a slow gentle tempo. Brian Jeffrey calls this melody a *strathspey*, which is a type of dance tune in common time, similar to a hornpipe but slower and more stately. The strathspey is striking for its "Scottish snaps" (a short note before a dotted note), which is generally exaggerated rhythmically for musical expression. The variations themselves, while attractive and technically challenging, don't sound particularly Scottish to me although the "snap" does return at the end.

Ye banks and braes o' bonnie Doon
How can ye bloom sae fresh and fair?
How can ye chaunt, ye little birds,
And I sae weary, fu' o' care.
Ye'll break my heart, ye warbling birds
That wanton through the flowery thorn,
Ye mind me o' departed joys,
Departed, never to return.

Oft hae I roved by bonnie Doon
To see the rose and woodbine twine,
And ilka bird sang o' its love,
And fondly sae did I o' mine.
Wi' lightsome heart I pu'd a rose
Fu' sweet upon its thorny tree
But my fause lover stole my rose,
And Ah! he left the thorn wi' me.

Elegiac Fantasy, Op. 59

The Elegiac Fantasy, Op. 59 is an elegy for the death of Charlotte Beslay, a talented former student of Sor's who died in childbirth. It was the penultimate composition that Sor wrote for the solo guitar and was probably composed around 1836 (three years before his own death.) A long Introduction leads into a Funeral March.

Towards the end of the piece the words "Charlotte, adieu!" are printed over a phrase of music. Some have wondered whether those words should be sung, or spoken, at that moment in the piece, but most players just keep the phrase in mind as a source of inspiration.

A Note About Fingerings

It should go without saying that almost all of the fingerings offered here are merely suggestions. While it is true that there are a few cases where a passage can only be managed by one particular fingering, it is far more often the case that a passage can be played in a variety of ways. The fingerings that I have selected for these pieces were chosen primarily with the intention to find a way to allow the guitarist to move between the chords ("shift") as smoothly and seamlessly as possible. Occasionally I chose fingerings that would bring out a color that I thought was attractive (often, for example, by putting the melody on the 2nd string instead of the 1st) but not if it made the piece substantially more difficult to play.

All that being said, I am constantly looking to improve my own fingerings and often change them. Even if you like these fingerings, it is a good idea to try other possibilities to see if you can find solutions that better suit your hands. At the very least, you will have stimulated your imagination by playing and hearing the piece in a different way. The best players never fully trust another player's fingerings. They are loyal instead to their own hands and ears. A less experienced player may have to temporarily lean on the suggestions of a veteran, but it is never too early to start experimenting on one's own. As Sor writes in his method, "I do not establish anything according to authority. You should not accept something just because your master did it rather, you should use reason to discover for yourself what the true principles are which underlie what you are examining."

A Note from the Publisher

We are proud to present *Alfred's Classical Guitar Masterworks Editions.* Our goal is to provide students and performers of the classical guitar the best possible editions of important repertoire with the editorial perspectives of great artists and teachers. The fingerings and other technical guides included in these scores will give you not only what may be new windows from which to view the pieces, but a new view into the thinking of these fine classical guitarists.

The pieces, of course, do not live on these pages. It is you who will breathe life into them and embue them with meaning. Thus, it is important that you learn everything you can about the composers and their intent, the styles and coventions of the periods and regions in which they were composed, and all of the formal aspects of their structures. A great performance is, among other things, well informed.

In the end, you must make your own choices about fingerings, articulations, dynamics, phrasing, etc., all of which are integrally related. Everything in the volume you're holding now is a respected classical guitarist's view of the music but I encourage you to dig deeper and go further—research, experiment, discuss, and become intimate with everything about the pieces you choose to study and perform. This is one of the great joys of being a musician: the music is not static; it lives and breathes in the work you do.

Thank you for including this edition in your study of this music.

–Nathaniel Gunod, Alfred Music

A Word of Thanks

Marc Teicholz and Alfred Music are grateful to Ed Burke, who played through and proofed the music in this collection.

This page intentionally left blank by the publisher.

Andante Largo

from Six Petite Pieces, Op. 5

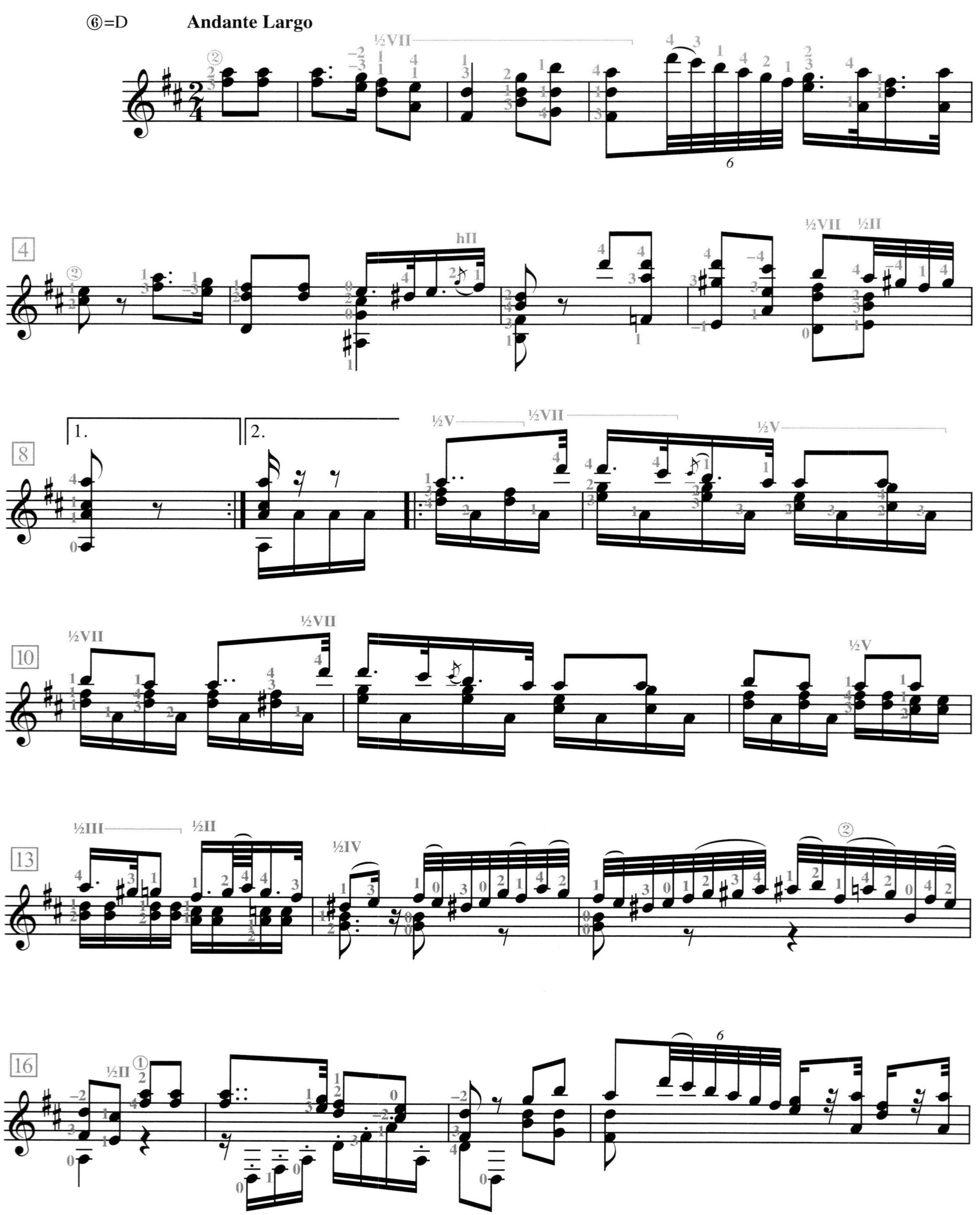

20
½III
½II
½VI
24
Mineur
½VII
28
½I
hII
I
32
I
III
½II
½III
½II
½I
36
40
½I

44
½III
Majeur
6
48
1.
52
2.
55
58
61
6
65
②

Largo

from Fantasy No. 2 in C Minor, Op. 7

* This ornament should be executed on the beat, with the G occuring simulaneously with the C and E♭

24
½VI
VI
27
VI
VI
30
III
III
33
III
36
IV
39
(IV)
I
42
I
f

* This harmonic can be played alternately as an artificial harmonic on the 10th fret of the 1st string.

Introduction & Variations on a Theme By Mozart, Op. 9

* These harmonics can be played with the RH in order to allow the chords to sustain longer.

* Bars 9–16 and 25–32 are alternate fingerings that can be used to create a contrast from the preceding section. You may choose, instead, to simply repeat the same fingerings twice.

28
½IX
1st
VARIATION
II
3
hI
6
8
11
14

* Bars 9–16 and 25–28 are alternate fingerings that can be used to create a contrast from the preceding section. You may choose, instead, to simply repeat the same fingerings twice.

29
3rd VARIATION
4
8
12
15

Più mosso
4th VARIATION
½IX

This page intentionally left blank by the publisher.
The 5th Variation is on the next page.

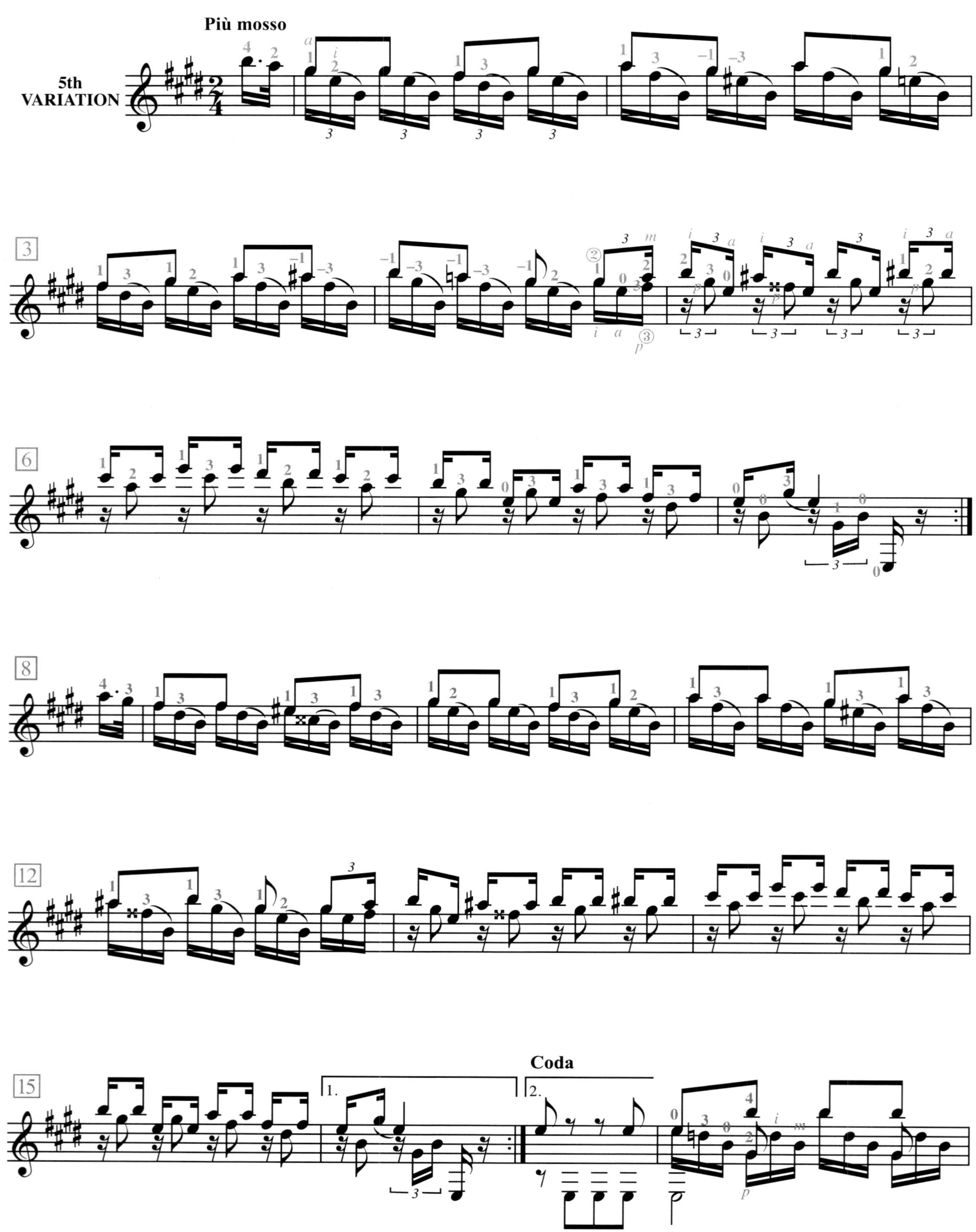
Più mosso
5th
VARIATION
Coda

18
½V
21
½V
½II
24
26
½IX
harm.
XII
30
34
½IX
VII

Sonata "Grand Solo" in D Major, Op. 14

* In measure 7 the grace notes come before the beat on the first chord and on the beat for the second chord (on beat 4).

** This ornament is executed on the beat (G♯ is simultaneous with the bass note A).

***

Ossia:
16
19
½VII
22
25
½III
28
½V
31
34
½V
½VII

37
½X
½V
②
½V
40
½VII
½IV
43
46
49
Ossia: 0 4 0 4 0
Ossia:
51
53

56
59
63
65
67
½VII
½V
Ossia:
70
72

74
76
79
Ossia:
82
85
½II
88

91
94
98
½VI
104
½VI
ff
p
107
110
112
114

116
½V
i m a
p
118
120
122
124
½I
pp
127
½I
f
I
hinge
130
(hinge)
p
I
f
p
133
f
½V
½VII

Ossia:
½X
½IV
½V
136
140
½V
Smorz. poco a poco
143
146
p
149
152
155

158
Ossia:
161
164
167
170
6
173
176

179
182
185
188
190
192
½V
(or 4)
(or 4)
II
* Julian Bream skips the next several bars of the piece by jumping from here to beat 2 of bar 211 and altering the meter for two bars:
187
211
then on to bar 212

195
½V
197
199
201
204
f
Ossia:
207

210
213
216
219
hinge
223
227
I
* Bream plays bars 220-221 and 224-225 like this:

** Bream repeats bars 235-238

Theme & Variations on the Folias and Minuet, Op. 15a

2nd
VARIATION

3rd
VARIATION
VII
IV
V
½V
4th
VARIATION
BVII
½II
½V

12
Andante
MINUET
5
9
13
17
21

Sonata in C Major, Op. 15b

* Can either be played as a grace note starting on beat 4 or as:

* This note can alternately be played on the 6th string with the fourth finger.

** Alternative RH fingering:

110
4/6I
113
½III
½II
116
III
120
III
124
128
132

164
167
171
I
III
175
III
179
183
186
VIII

Introduction & Variations on "Marlborough s'en va-t-en guerre," Op. 28

9
13
½II
17
½III
1st VARIATION
4
8
½VII
½V

12
16
Andantino mineur
2nd VARIATION
4
13
17

Tempo primo major
3rd VARIATION
½II
½VII
5
½II
½V
½VII
½V
harm.
V
harm.
IV
harm.
III
13
17
½VII

4th
VARIATION
4
8
12
16

5th
VARIATION
½II
3
5
7
½II
½II
½V
½VII
9
11
13

15
17
19
½VII
22
25
½VI
27
harm.
VII
harm.
XII
harm.
IX
harm.
V
harm.
III
p
33
½I
II
harm.
IV
harm.
V
harm.
V
harm.
V
harm.
IV

Fantasy & Variations on the Scottish Air "Ye Banks and Braes," Op. 40

THEME
3
7
11
15

1st
VARIATION
½II
½II
½V
½VII
Fine
½V
½VII
½VII
D.S. al Fine

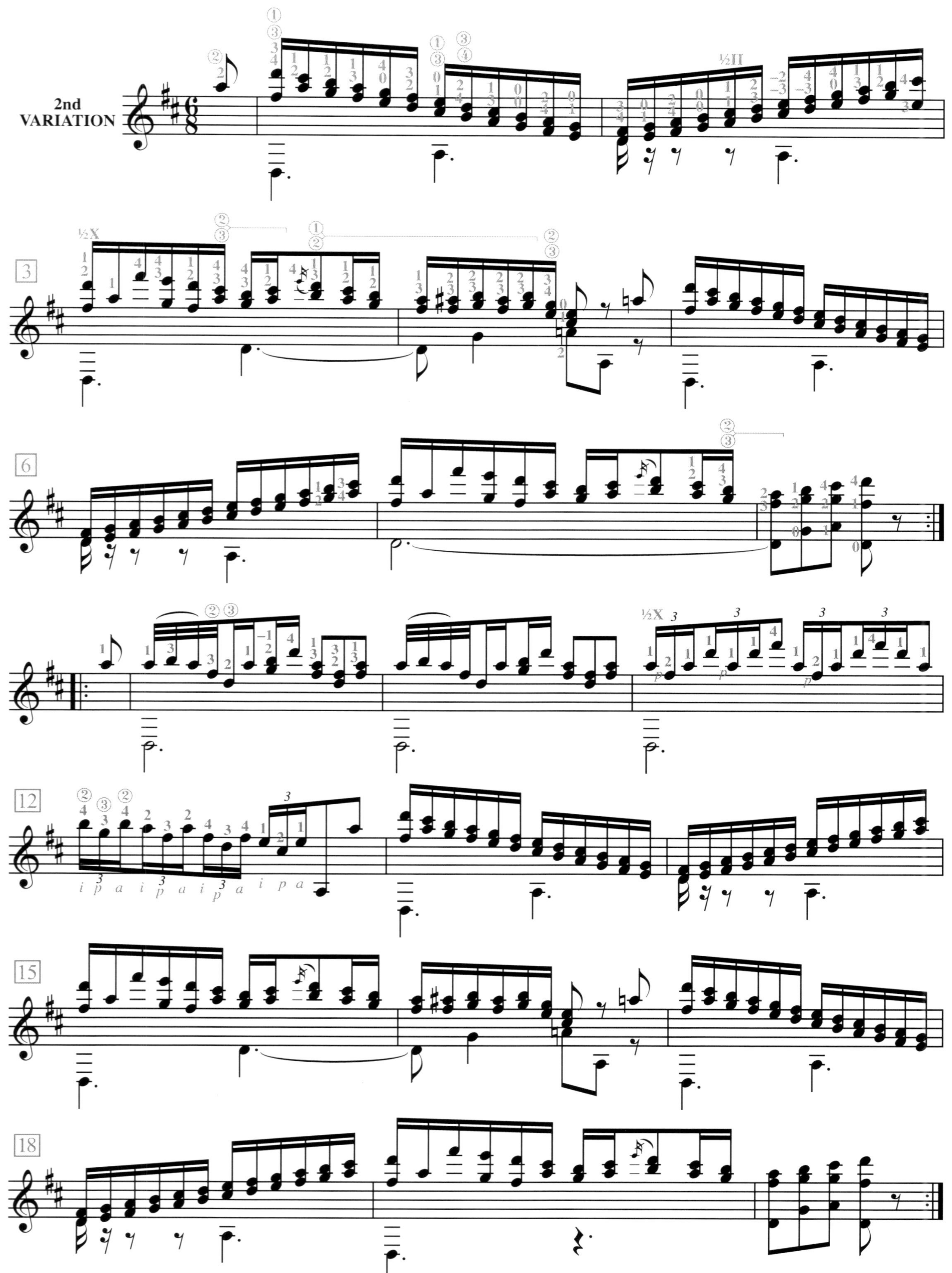
2nd
VARIATION
½II
½X
3
6
12
15
18

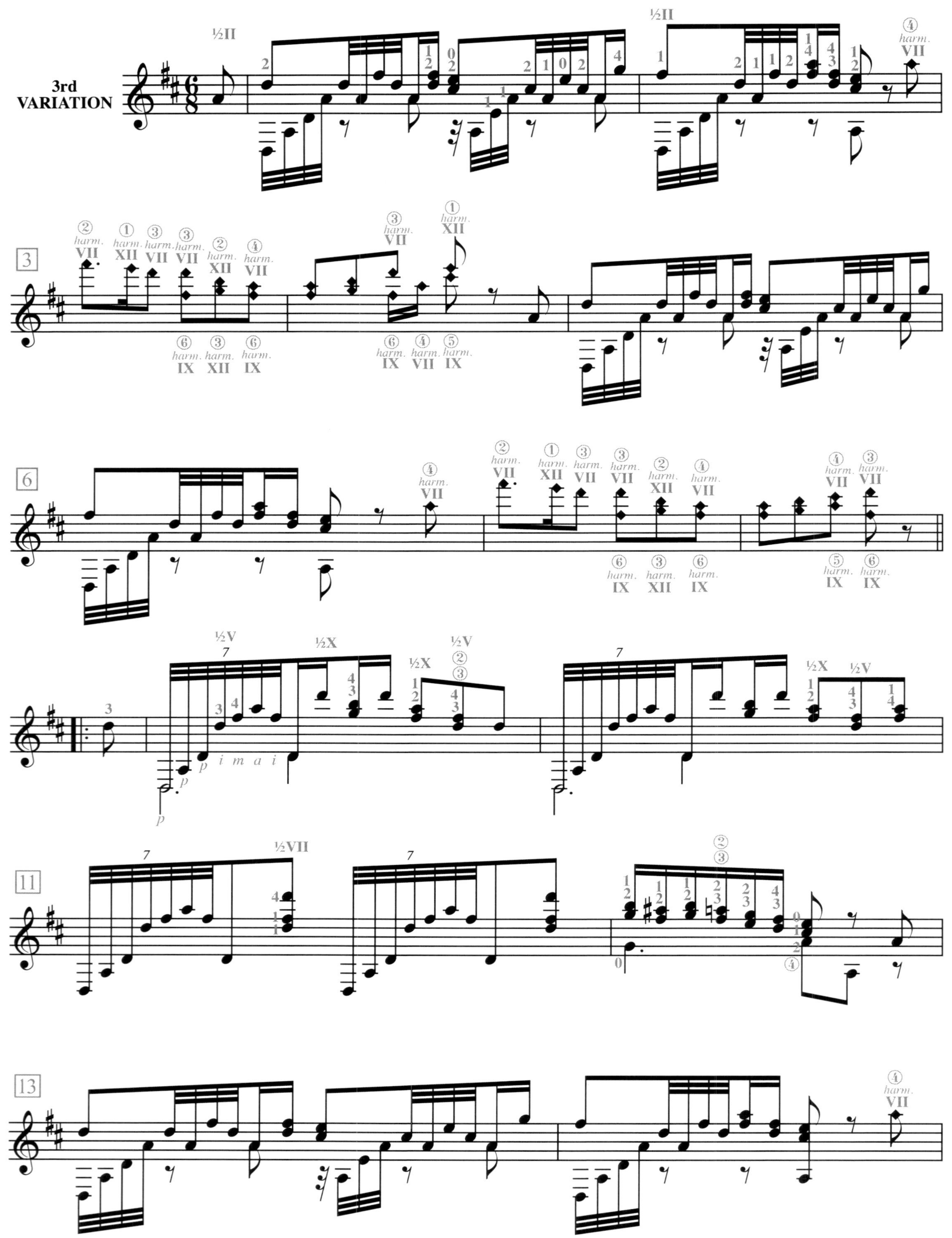
3rd
VARIATION
harm.
p i m a i
p

Elegiac Fantasy, Op. 59

26
cresc.
marcando
29
33
37
40
43
46

49
52
55
58
61
63
66
IV
V
½V
½II
III

70
74
78
82
86
90
94

97
101
½V
104
108
pp
ff
½II
p
113
cres
cen
do
116
½V
½IV
119
½VII
½VI

122
½V
½IV
½V
125
128
130
132
134
137
VII
dolce
f
dolce
f
p
dim.

FUNERAL MARCH
VII
harm.
XII
½IV
½V
II
½II
IV

50
54
58
62
harm.
XII
66
69
72

76
½I
80
III
f
84
dolce
88
pp
Charlotte!
92
Adieu!
III
più f
p
96
harm.
XII
harm.
VII
pp